Quantum Leap
Understanding How Quantum Teleportation Works

Table of Contents

Chapter 1. Introduction

Welcome to a journey that will take us to the frontiers of human understanding, where the lines of science and wonder blur. Our Special Report, "Quantum Leap: Understanding How Quantum Teleportation Works," brings you to the thrilling heart of quantum mechanics without requiring you to be a seasoned physicist. It strips away the perplexing jargon and complex mathematics to provide an enlightening overview of quantum teleportation, an area of science that sounds like science fiction but is a startling reality. With this report, we will bridge the gap between the abstractly complex and the intriguingly simple. Discover this spellbinding world where particles can be in two places at once, information travels faster than light, and teleportation isn't just for the movies. This beckoning adventure awaits both curious minds and daring spirits. Take the leap with us; you'll be amazed by the reality that science uncovers.

Chapter 2. The Quantum Realm: An Introduction

Quantum mechanics has been the cornerstone of modern physics since its inception in the early 20th century. It depicts the universe in ways that seem highly unintuitive, dealing with phenomena on the tiniest scales of atoms and subatomic particles. It is the basis of the digital devices we use every day, the computers servicing our internet, and potentially, the future of all technology through quantum computing and quantum teleportation.

First, let's lay down some groundwork. The universe, as we perceive it at the macroscopic level, operates under a set of physical laws known as classical mechanics, formulated by Sir Isaac Newton. It's predictable; if you throw a ball up into the air, you know it will come down. However, when we go down to the atomic and subatomic level, these rules fail spectacularly and a new set of rules is needed: the quantum rules.

2.1. The Wave-Particle Duality

The quantum world is a maze, filled with seemingly paradoxical phenomena. One such peculiar behavior is the wave-particle duality. Until the advent of quantum physics, the world was simple: light was a wave, and matter consisted of particles. However, experiments like the double-slit experiment showed that particles like electrons exhibited wave-like behavior, creating interference patterns. Moreover, light could also behave as a stream of particles known as photons.

2.2. The Uncertainty Principle

Another oddity that resides in the quantum realm is the Uncertainty

Principle, introduced by Werner Heisenberg in 1927. It states that you cannot, no matter the precision of your measuring tools, simultaneously measure both the position and velocity of a subatomic particle with total certainty. In other words, the more precisely you try to measure a particle's position, the less precisely you can know its velocity, and vice versa.

2.3. Quantum Superposition

One of the cornerstones of quantum physics is the principle of superposition. It suggests that quantum particles can exist in multiple states simultaneously, only settling down into a single state once observed or measured.

Consider the famous thought experiment by Schrödinger's cat. The cat is simultaneously in a superposition of both alive and dead states until we observe it, leading to a collapsed definite state of either alive or dead. In broader terms, this paradox addresses the difference between the quantum microworld's probabilistic nature and our macro-world's definite one.

2.4. Quantum Entanglement

Arguably one of the most 'spooky' concepts in quantum physics is the effect of quantum entanglement. Once two quantum particles become enmeshed or 'entangled,' they can instantly affect one another's state, no matter how far apart they are. If you change the state of one entangled particle, the other changes simultaneously. This immediate action seems to defy a cornerstone of Einstein's relativity – the limit of the speed of light.

2.5. Quantum Teleportation: A Glimpse

Harnessing and manipulating the concepts of quantum superposition and entanglement, scientists have made impressive progress in teleporting quantum information. It's important to make clear that this teleportation doesn't resemble classical teleportation seen in sci-fi films. It doesn't involve the disappearance and reappearance of physical objects. Instead, the information about the quantum state of a particle disappears from its original location and simultaneously appears at another, irrespective of the distance.

The universe we thought we knew, the one governed by straightforward laws, becomes a sea of possibilities and probabilities at its most fundamental levels – the quantum realm. Unveiling these quantum world mysteries are not just scientific quests; they are philosophical endeavors. They communicate to us that the universe is grander, stranger, and more beautiful than we could possibly imagine.

Perseverance in this enigmatic realm has revealed fruitful results that conflict with common sense but align with rigorous experimentations. As quantum mechanics continues to unveil its bewildering nature, it encourages a deeper investigation into the secrets of our universe, leading to encouraging technological leaps blurring the boundary between science and magic.

Navigating the vast seas of quantum mechanics is as thrilling as explorations into the deep abyss of oceans or the soaring heights of the cosmos. Equipped with an understanding of the basic concepts of quantum mechanics such as wave-particle duality, the uncertainty principle, quantum superposition, and quantum entanglement, we are now ready to dive deeper into the astonishing world of quantum teleportation. With a blend of patience, curiosity, and a bit of quantum courage, the bizarre quantum realm's enthralling secrets will unravel into meaningful, tangible realities.

Chapter 3. Unlocking the Quantum Paradox

The allure of the quantum world stems from the astonishing phenomena it presents, laws that convolutely defy our everyday intuition. One of these bewildering occurrences is the quantum paradox, a mystery that permeates quantum mechanics and proves challenging to reconcile with classical physics.

In an attempt to explore these mysterious paradoxes, let's start with the fundamental essence of quantum mechanics.

3.1. The Dance of Particles

Quantum mechanics is the study of particles at the atomic and subatomic level. Unlike the objects we interact with in our day-to-day lives, these particles behave in ways that can often seem strange and inconsistent to us. That's because they abide by their own rules—rules that are, in essence, quantum mechanics.

Rather than maintaining fixed properties, as a tennis ball or a car might, quantum particles exist in a state of uncertainty, or "superposition." In other words, they can exist in multiple states simultaneously until those states are observed or measured, much like Schrödinger's infamous cat, which is both alive and dead until observed.

3.2. Entanglement: A Quantum Love Story

A key feature of quantum paradoxes is entanglement, described by Albert Einstein as "spooky action at a distance." Two particles can become entangled, meaning the state of one instantaneously influences the state of the other, regardless of the distances separating them, defying the classical physical limit of information transfer, the speed of light. Such behavior contradicts our intuitive understanding of the universe.

3.3. The Double Slit Experiment

Now that we're somewhat familiar with superposition and entanglement, let's delve into a classical experiment, known as the double-slit experiment.

When particles, such as photons or electrons, are fired towards a barrier with two slits, something peculiar happens. Rather than behaving as particles and going through one slit or the other, they behave as waves. This results in an interference pattern on a screen behind the barrier—the kind you would expect to see from a light wave being split and then recombining.

However, this strange occurrence only happens if we don't observe which slit the particle goes through. When we introduce a detector to monitor the photons' pathways, each photon suddenly behaves as a particle again, resulting in two strips of light on the screen as if they had passed through one slit or the other, indicating a collapsed wave function.

This experiment underpins the weirdness of the quantum world—particles behaving as waves when not observed but as particles when observed. This is quantum superposition is at play and is pivotal in understanding quantum paradox.

3.4. Wave-Particle Duality and the Measurement Problem

In the realm of quantum mechanics, particles also exhibit what is known as wave-particle duality. They behave as both localized particles and as spread-out waves. It sounds counter-intuitive because in our daily lives, we never see a soccer ball dribbling itself or a wave suddenly becoming a particle.

What perplexes scientists further is the measurement problem. Why does observation cause a quantum system to drop its various probabilities and decide on just one outcome—collapsing its wave function? A leading interpretation of quantum mechanics, the Copenhagen interpretation, suggests that the act of observation itself forces the particle to resolve its multiple states into one. Quantum paradox, then, represents this core challenge of reconciling superposition, wave-particle duality, and the impact of measurement.

3.5. Localization, Globalization and the Role of Decoherence

Yet one more paradox in the quantum world relates to the localization of quantum states. We can't assign specific locations to electrons orbiting a nucleus, yet we can accurately define its global presence around the nucleus.

Decoherence, however, helps us bridge the peculiar quantum behavior and the understandable classical world. Interaction of a quantum system with its environment causes the system to lose its quantum behavior—superposition, and entanglement—over time and behave more classically, a phenomenon known as quantum decoherence.

However, in extreme conditions, like at temperatures near absolute zero, coherent quantum behaviors can be maintained for longer times, opening avenues to technologies like quantum computing and quantum teleportation.

In conclusion, quantum paradox, central to quantum mechanics, is not about the impossible, but rather the unimaginably strange.

Quantum paradoxes stem from the laws of the quantum world, laws that govern the building blocks of reality itself but appear alien to our macroscopic reality. Unlocking these paradoxes helps us understand and venture deeper into this fascinating, mind-boggling reality.

Though Einstein was never comfortable with the quantum leap, it's through such leaps that we've come to grasp the paradoxes and develop technologies on the brink of another revolution. The powerful quantum paradox, thus, holds the key to our immensely bright, albeit uncertain, quantum future.

Chapter 4. Teleportation: From Fiction to Physics

Quantum teleportation challenges our everyday understanding of the world we live in, mixing a pallet of mind-bending physics and mind-boggling futurism that transports us into the surreal realm typically associated with psychedelic dreams or science-fiction movies.

4.1. The Concept of Teleportation

The idea of "teleportation" is not new. It has been a common theme in many science fiction stories for decades, like Arthur C. Clarke's 'The City and the Stars' or the 'Star Trek' series where the crew effectively evaporates and rematerializes on a foreign planet or spaceship. How sublime would it be if we could actually beam our physical bodies across space instantly, without facing the torment of traffic jams or grueling transatlantic flights. But can this stunning idea break the shackles of fiction and venture into the realm of reality?

Teleportation, from a purely physical perspective, requires the exact reconstruction of an object at a distant location, and quantum mechanics provides a theoretical grounding for this in the form of quantum teleportation.

4.2. Quantum Mechanics and Teleportation

The bedrock of quantum teleportation is quantum entanglement, an uncanny phenomenon first proposed by Einstein, Podolsky, and Rosen in 1935, who called it 'spooky action at a distance.' Quantum entanglement dictates that two quantum states can become interlinked such that the state of one would instantly determine the other, regardless of the spatial separation.

Digging deeper into quantum entanglement, we find the principle of superposition, saying that a quantum particle can exist in many states simultaneously until it's observed or measured. Only at that point does it 'choose' a state in which to exist. Imagine running errands in several places at once and then magically finishing all your tasks when someone checks up on you.

So, how does this mind-boggling realm of quantum physics relate to teleportation? In 1993, scientists Bennett, Brassard, Crepeau, Jozsa, Peres, and Wootters, discovered a process to teleport quantum information. Known as the BCPW protocol, it enables transmission of exact quantum states from one location to another, using entanglement and classical communication channels. But beware! No physical entity is transported; only the information about a quantum state is teleported.

4.3. Quantum Teleportation in Action

Now, let's delve deeper into the quantum teleportation process. Imagine we have two entangled particles, particle A and particle B. Particle A is with user Alice while particle B is with user Bob. Alice also possesses an additional particle, say C, the state of which she desires to teleport to Bob.

Alice performs a bell-state measurement on particles A and C. The result, combined with the previously known entangled state of particles A and B, allows Bob, via some classical communication method, to infer the quantum state of particle C and apply the necessary transformation to his particle B. Thus, particle B adopts the original state of particle C, effectively teleporting the information. Fascinatingly though, transferring the information in this way doesn't mean the transfer of any material substance. Instead, the transported information is used to reconstruct the quantum state at the receiving end.

4.4. Quantum Teleportation in Practice

In recent years, scientists have successfully demonstrated quantum teleportation. In 2017, Chinese researchers teleported a photon from Earth to an orbiting satellite over 1400km away, pushing the boundaries of quantum teleportation to an unprecedented distance. Meanwhile, a team from the University of Calgary teleported a small light particle 6.2 kilometers across their city using a dedicated optical fibre network.

These experiments showcase the burgeoning potential of quantum teleportation, especially for quantum communication and computing applications. To put it in perspective, the quantum internet, predicted to be the next evolution of the web, would include secure communication protocols impervious to eavesdropping due to the fundamental properties of quantum mechanics.

In conclusion, quantum teleportation signifies an extraordinary leap from fiction to physics. Like unravelling a mystery novel, every advancement strips away a layer of the unknown, providing an exhilarating glance at the future potentials that gleam beyond the realm of our current understanding. The lines between science fiction and reality are blurring, making quantum teleportation an area of science that's equal parts intriguing, stupefying, and wonderfully disruptive.

Chapter 5. The Quantum Entanglement Phenomenon

Let's delve into the heart of Quantum Mechanics, one of the most enigmatic realms of physics that has confounded and fascinated scientists for more than a century. More than any other theory, Quantum Mechanics challenges our understanding of the universe. And one cornerstone of this theory is the wonderfully strange phenomenon of Quantum Entanglement.

5.1. Quantum Entanglement: An Introduction

Quantum entanglement is a physical phenomenon that occurs when pairs or groups of particles interact in ways such that the quantum state of each particle cannot be described independently—instead, a quantum state may be given for the system as a whole.

Mathematically speaking, the properties of entangled particles are more strongly correlated than classical physics would allow. This correlation holds regardless of the distance separating the particles—it can be an inch or across galaxies.

To comprehend quantum entanglement, imagine two entangled particles, Particle A and Particle B. Regardless of how far they are placed from each other, measuring a property, like spin, on Particle A instantly determines the corresponding property on Particle B. Remarkably, this transfer of information happens instantaneously, seemingly faster than the speed of light.

5.2. From Simple Systems to Entangled Particles

To understand quantum entanglement, it is crucial to take a detour through the simpler scenario of individual quantum particles. Conceptually, a quantum particle can exist in a superposition of states. This principle holds for any measurable physical property, like position, momentum or spin. In a superposed state, the particle does not have a definite value for these properties until they are measured.

In our daily experience, flipping a coin offers us a chance to encounter a superposition-like state, where we can only predict probabilities or chance of the final outcome. Unlike a spinning coin, however, a quantum particle stays in superposition until measurement. According to the Copenhagen interpretation of Quantum Mechanics, the act of measuring a property forces the particle to 'choose' one definite state, uniquely determined by the probabilities described by its superposition.

When dealing with entangled particles, this concept of superposition moves up a level. It is not each particle that is in superposition but the system of particles. Take our pair of particles again, Particle A and Particle B. Before measurement, each particle does not have a definite spin—it could be either up or down, and it's as if each particle is in a superposition of both. But measurement immediately determines the spin state of both particles, even if they are light years apart.

5.3. The EPR Paradox and Bell's Theorem

The spooky action at a distance, as Albert Einstein once referred to quantum entanglement, led Einstein, Podolsky, and Rosen (EPR) to propose the EPR paradox. They argued in their 1935 paper that the Quantum Mechanics description of the physical world, in its current form, was incomplete. It assumed the presence of hidden variables that if discovered, could explain these instant correlations without defying the speed of light limit of Einstein's theory of Relativity.

Responding to the EPR paradox, physicist John Bell devised a groundbreaking theorem in 1964, popularly known as Bell's theorem, taking the alleged issue head-on. Bell's theorem presented experimental setups and inequalities (known as Bell's inequalities) that could distinguish between a quantum world and one with local hidden variables as proposed by EPR.

Experiments have consistently violated Bell's inequalities, validating the Quantum Mechanics prediction and suggesting that the Universe, at its core, is highly non-local or interconnected. It led to the scientific acceptance that nature is fundamentally probabilistic and the concepts of quantum entanglement adequately describe correlations between particles, no matter how unsettling these concepts may seem.

5.4. Quantum Entanglement in Technology

Aside from its theoretical importance, Quantum Entanglement holds massive potential for technological advancements, particularly in industries like computing and cryptography.

Quantum computers, utilizing quantum bits or qubits, leverage entanglement to perform multiple complex calculations simultaneously. Such a quantum superposition of states leads to an exponential surge in computing power. Qubits interconnected through entanglement provide the basis for quantum algorithms, potentially revolutionizing the field of quantum computing.

Quantum cryptography, utilizing entanglement, allows the creation of unbreakable encryption codes. Any attempt to intercept communication would disrupt the entangled state, revealing the intrusion and preserving the security of the information.

Quantum teleportation, which involves the transmission of quantum information, leveraging entanglement, stands as an active research area promising radical changes in how we approach communication. Although significant challenges remain, including maintaining entangled states over long distances, a quantum internet seems closer to reality than ever before.

5.5. Conclusion: The Persistent Enigma

Quantum entanglement resides at the core of the quantum world, defying our deeply ingrained intuitions and challenging our understanding of reality. Born as a suspect oddity, entanglement has traveled a long path to earn its recognition as an actual physical phenomenon and a carrier of technological potential. It displays the distinctive feature of quantum interconnectivity that sets Quantum Mechanics apart from classical physics.

Yet, quantum entanglement remains shrouded with numerous unanswered questions and doubts. As we advance deeper into the 21st century, gaining a better understanding of this enigma promises not only to reveal more about our universe but also to pave the way for revolutionary technologies built on the principles of quantum mechanics.

And so, the quantum leap continues. The universe, as seen through the quantum lens, emerges not as a collection of individual, distinctly functioning parts, but as a confusingly entangled, inseparable whole. Perhaps, like quantum particles, we need to exist in a superposed state of mind—of fascination, bewilderment, anticipation and acceptance—ever ready to embrace the quantum dance of reality.

Chapter 6. Quantum Teleportation: The Key Concepts

The phenomenon of quantum teleportation will seem like an alien concept, especially to those not familiar with the quantum realm. However, it is a purely physical process based on the principles of quantum mechanics, one of the most successful theories of modern physics. Let's venture into this mind-boggling world, but first, let's take a moment to build a foundation in quantum mechanics - a necessary step to truly appreciate the magic and mystery of quantum teleportation.

6.1. Quantum Mechanics - The Pillar of Quantum Teleportation

Quantum mechanics is the scientific theory that provides a description of nature at its most fundamental level, the level of elementary particles. The theory predictably describes the behaviors of particles such as electrons and photons - the basic units of matter and light, respectively.

At the heart of quantum mechanics are two key principles: superposition and entanglement.

6.1.1. Superposition

If asked, 'Is the light on or off?' the immediate expectation is a straightforward answer: either 'on' or 'off.' However, in quantum mechanics, the possibilities are significantly more nuanced. An object governed by quantum rules could be in multiple states at once, thanks to the concept called superposition. It implies that a quantum system can exist in multiple states simultaneously, but once observed, it will collapse to one deterministic condition.

For example, imagine a quantum particle that can exist in state A or B. According to superposition, the particle is in both state A and state B simultaneously until we measure it.

6.1.2. Quantum Entanglement

The second key principle is Quantum Entanglement, where the state of two or more particles becomes inseparably linked, no matter their distance apart. Changes to the state of one will instantaneously impact the other(s). Albert Einstein dubbed this "spooky action at a distance."

With this foundational knowledge, we can now explore the principle of quantum teleportation.

6.2. Journey Into Quantum Teleportation

Quantum teleportation does not involve any physical movement in space-time as conventional meaning of teleportation might suggest. Rather, it is a process by which quantum information (e.g., the exact state of an atom or photon) is transmitted from one place to another, without traversing the physical space connecting them. The process is deeply rooted in the principles of superposition and quantum entanglement.

6.2.1. The Mechanism of Quantum Teleportation

Usually, quantum teleportation involves three parties – Alice, Bob, and Charlie. Alice is the sender, and Bob is the receiver. Charlie holds an entangled pair of particles, sends one to Alice while keeping the other with him.

The process then occurs as follows:

1. Alice prepares the particle she wants to teleport and describes its unknown quantum state (Ψ).

2. Charlie sends Alice one particle of the entangled pair.

3. Alice then performs a joint measurement on her original particle and the received entangled particle, collapsing the superposition.

4. The measurement results are sent to Bob (via classical communication).

5. When Bob applies the necessary transformation based on the received details, the unknown quantum state (Ψ) is reproduced by Bob's particle.

It is pivotal to understand that it's not the original particle that gets teleported but the information it carries with it. It's also important to note the role of classical communication. Without it, Bob would end up with a particle in some quantum state, but he wouldn't know which one.

6.2.2. No Cloning Theorem

A natural question would be, why doesn't Alice simply copy the quantum state and send it to Bob? This question leads us to the No-Cloning theorem, another principle of quantum mechanics. Simply stated, this principle tells us that it's impossible to make an exact copy of an arbitrary unknown quantum state - a rule that, in turn, preserves the integrity of quantum information and quantum communication.

6.3. Quantum Teleportation - A Reality

Quantum teleportation is no longer theoretical. Scientists have gradually made it a reality.

In 1997, a group of scientists performed the first successful quantum teleportation experiment. They successfully teleported a photon across a one-meter distance. Since then, various experiments have been conducted, each pushing the boundary and teleporting quantum information over increasing distances.

A record was set by Chinese scientists in 2017 when they managed to teleport a photon from the Earth to a satellite orbiting 500 kilometers above, using a process called quantum teleportation.

Strides in quantum teleportation demonstrate its practicality, particularly in the field of quantum communication, where it holds the promise of perfect security based on the principles of quantum mechanics.

To consider quantum teleportation as magical would be an injustice, it's not an illusion, but a real, established process based on the principles of quantum mechanics. As we uncover more and more about this exciting area of research, the boundary of our understanding continues to expand, bringing us a step closer to a future where teleportation could well become a part of our daily life.

This adventure is one of intrigue, suspense, and discovery. The principles behind quantum teleportation are challenging to accept and yet statistically undeniable. As we dive deeper, our preconceived notions of reality are questioned, and we find ourselves in a realm of science that often seems stranger than fiction. Yet, it is in this complexity, we find beauty and a deeper connection to the reality surrounding us - the reality that is captivated by the spell of quantum mechanics.

Though these subjects are complex, they are not insurmountable. As explorers on the precipice of understanding, our journey together doesn't stop here. Quantum teleportation is just the beginning. Welcome to a world where seeing is not always believing, where understanding replaces the need for belief, and where only question left after reaching the edge of understanding is: "What's next?"

Chapter 7. Crypto-Algorithms & Quantum Computers: The Connection

The transformational catalyst known as quantum computing derives its magnificent power from the peculiar laws of quantum mechanics. These laws govern the behavior of subatomic particles, enabling computers to take on tasks considered unfeasible by today's standards. Particles governed by quantum mechanics can exist in multiple states simultaneously and become entangled, meaning their properties interconnect despite distance. Quantum computing utilizes these phenomena, potentially revolutionizing fields like cryptography, where formidable challenges persist. This promises a future where classical encryption codes could either be effortlessly shattered or become impenetrable.

7.1. The Landscape of Cryptography

The burgeoning domain of cryptography involves disguising information to protect it from unintended recipients. Commonly, it operates by converting readable data (plaintext) into encrypted text (ciphertext) using mathematical algorithms and a key. In essence, cryptography can be conceptualized as an unbreakable lock, with the encryption algorithm serving as the lock and the key used to encode the data providing the unlocking mechanism.

The strength of a cryptographic algorithm depends on two elements: its inherent mathematical structure and the length of the key used. The race to ensure continued security in the quantum era has led to the development of new cryptographic techniques.

However, let's first explore common crypto-algorithms that hold together the fabric of our digital interactions.

7.1.1. Symmetric and Asymmetric Encryption

Symmetric encryption, also known as secret key encryption, employs the same key for encryption and decryption. Both parties must have the key, raising the issue of secure key transmission. Some of its most prevalent algorithms include DES, 3DES, AES, and RC4, the latter being the backbone for SSL and TLS security layers.

Unlike symmetric encryption, asymmetric encryption uses a pair of keys for encryption and decryption: a public key available to everyone and a private key that remains secret. The RSA (Rivest-Shamir-Adleman) algorithm is the most prevalent form of asymmetric encryption.

7.2. Quantum Computers and Classical Crypto-Algorithms

These prevailing crypto-algorithms, though robust against classical attacks, are exceedingly vulnerable to quantum computing. The function underpinning asymmetric algorithms is the factorization of large numbers, a process markedly expedited by quantum computers.

7.2.1. Shor's Algorithm: The Cryptographic Nightmare

In 1994, mathematician Peter Shor formulated an algorithm that exploits quantum computing's potential to solve factorization problems exponentially faster than classical computers. If quantum devices become scalable and robust, Shor's algorithm could decode RSA encryption in seconds, shattering the internet's foremost security barrier.

7.3. Post-Quantum Cryptography

To withstand the potential quantum threat, a new cryptographic paradigm called post-quantum cryptography is emerging. These encryption methods strive to resist quantum attacks while remaining feasible for current machines.

7.3.1. Lattice-Based Cryptography

Some of the most promising post-quantum algorithms are based on lattice problems, mathematical challenges believed to resist both classical and quantum attacks. Lattice issues revolve around locating the closest point in a grid of multi-dimensional points, a problem not expedited by quantum computing.

7.3.2. Code-Based Cryptography

Code-based cryptography is another prominent contender. Its principal algorithm, McEliece, was formulated in 1978 and has withstood both quantum and classical attacks. It uses error-correcting codes to create secure encryption, presenting an arduous challenge for quantum computers.

7.3.3. Multivariate Cryptography

Multivariate cryptography, embodying encryption based on multivariate polynomial equations, is another promising field. The degree of difficulty in solving these equations presents a daunting challenge for both classical and quantum computers.

7.4. The Advent of Quantum Cryptography

While post-quantum cryptography serves as an impenetrable shield, quantum cryptography emerges as an essential sword. Unlike traditional encryption relying on mathematical complexity, quantum cryptography is grounded in the laws of physics, making it immune to any computational advancements.

7.4.1. Quantum Key Distribution (QKD)

The most revolutionary application of quantum cryptography is Quantum Key Distribution (QKD). By utilizing the quantum properties of photons, two users can share a cryptographic key, with any act of eavesdropping disturbing the quantum state and thereby alerting the users.

In this extraordinary journey, we're faced with the reality that quantum computers behold both promise and peril. They're potential tools for decoding classical encryption, yet they also present a dawn of unprecedentedly secure encryption methods. With the rise of quantum algorithms, both old and new cryptographic methods are transforming, paving the way for an enthralling era of security and secrecy.

Chapter 8. Quantum Teleportation Experiments: Successes and Obstacles

Max Planck, a giant in the world of physics, once famously quipped, "Science cannot solve the ultimate mystery of nature." One might argue that quantum teleportation is a key part of that enigmatic puzzle. To unravel it, scientists over time have embarked on various experimental pursuits, each with its own share of triumphs and challenges.

8.1. The Principle and Experimentation History of Quantum Teleportation

Born from theoretical birth in the 1990s, quantum teleportation is a fascinating process by which quantum information, such as the state of an atom or photon, can be transmitted from one location to another without any physical link. This concept materialized in experimental form for the first time in 1997, when a group of physicists from the University of Innsbruck succeeded in teleporting photons over a distance of about one meter.

In 2004, the same team achieved teleportation with atoms, verifying the promise of quantum teleportation. This series of successes drew increasing attention to the possibilities of quantum teleportation. However, these advancements aren't exactly similar to relocating objects or humans—the essence of teleportation in science fiction. Instead, it's about transferring the properties (or state) between particles, no matter their distance apart.

8.2. What Makes Quantum Teleportation Unique

The element that sets quantum teleportation apart is a bizarre phenomenon called quantum entanglement. A fundamental part of the quantum world, entanglement involves a pair (or more) particles being so intrinsically linked that they reflect each other's states instantaneously across any distance. This peculiar connection doesn't abide by the conventional speed limit of the universe – the speed of light.

The process starts with quantum entanglement of a pair of particles, one of which then interacts with the particle to be teleported. Subsequent measurement of the pair's state forces it into one of many possible states, subsequently affecting the distant entangled particle instantaneously. This measurement is then transmitted to the receiver via traditional communication means, where the receiver applies a 'correction' to their entangled particle based on the state information, thus recreating the original state of the particle at their end. This way, the particle's state has effectively 'teleported' from the sender to the receiver.

8.3. Teleportation of Quantum Information: Success Stories

Recalling the history of quantum teleportation experiments, the first attempt of demonstrating this mysterious physical phenomenon took place in 1997, and it was a significant success for quantum mechanics. Under the guidance of physicists at the University of Innsbruck in Austria, the state of a photon was teleported over distances of about a meter.

In an even more exciting development, two quantum teleportation records were broken in 2012. Chinese physicists achieved teleportation over 97km across a lake, proving its feasibility over sizeable earthly distances. Soon after, the European Space Agency reported successful teleportation between the ground and a satellite revolving the earth.

The field of quantum information and communication has hit more landmarks since then. In 2015, researchers managed to quantum teleport information across a city's fiber network over a distance of 7km.

One of the most momentous experiments conducted in recent history was by two teams from Calgary, Canada, and Hefei, China, independently. Both succeeded in teleporting a photon many kilometers, 8.2 km and 10 km, respectively, tackling significant topological and atmospheric challenges.

Turning from photons to heavier particles, researchers reported the teleportation of the quantum state of a proton to another for the first time in 2004. For their experiment, the Austrian team, led by the group that pioneered quantum teleportation seven years earlier, chose beryllium ions. The protons' quantum states were successfully teleported, showing that quantum information could be moved around in larger, composite objects.

8.4. Challenges and Obstacles in Quantum Teleportation Experiments

Despite the incredible strides made in the study and application of quantum teleportation, the journey is paved with obstacles. In real-world aspects, the long-distance teleportation of quantum information is still in infancy, mainly due to the challenge we face in maintaining entanglement over large distances. Due to 'decoherence', a kind of noise in quantum systems, the delicate state of entanglement more often than not degrades over extended distances.

Furthermore, quantum teleportation experiments are instrumentally challenging, requiring perfect synchronization between the sender and the receiver — a daunting task over large distances and through different atmospheric conditions. Also, with our current technology, the data transferred during Quantum Teleportation is very sparse.

When quantum teleportation is eventually scaled up from the quantum regime to the classical world - physically larger systems—things get a lot trickier. The manipulation and preservation of quantum states become more difficult as systems scale up, making the prospect of teleporting larger objects a far-reaching goal.

8.5. Amidst Doubts and Skepticism: The Future of Quantum Teleportation

Undeterred by obstacles, the scientific community continues to forge ahead, buoyed by significant developments such as Quantum Internet, which has been theorized to use quantum entanglement to send information. In a quantum internet, quantum teleportation will be the primary method of transporting information, potentially enabling secure communication, ultra-fast communication speed, and quantum computing across large networks.

Moreover, research into the teleportation of complex, composite systems, such as biological systems, has begun, with a study on teleporting the quantum states of a bacterium and a mirror-reporting positive results. If we can maintain the integrity of the quantum state in these complex systems, a new world of applications opens.

Despite the skepticism and doubt concerning quantum teleportation, its reality challenges us to confront our understanding of the universe and its boundaries. It underscores the necessity of continuing to advance our knowledge and understanding. Despite the difficulties we may face now or in the future, the unraveling of this quantum puzzle could lead to unparalleled leaps in technological advancements, making the impossible, possible. Developing a more profound understanding of quantum teleportation is key to unlocking a new era in science based on the principles of quantum mechanics. With every success and failure, we come closer to the day when quantum teleportation becomes as common in our lives as sending a text message.

Chapter 9. The Future of Quantum Teleportation: Possibilities & Challenges

As we peer into the farthest reaches of scientific understanding, we stand on the precipice of the world's next transformative leap in communication and computation. Quantum teleportation, still a burgeoning field, promises breathtaking prospects that could turn many paradigms of our current understanding upside down once they are fully realized. In this adventure into the future, we will gaze into the possibilities of what might be and the challenges we must overcome to get there.

9.1. The Dawn of Quantum Internet

Imagine an Internet with no possibility of a security breach, seemingly instantaneous communication regardless of distance, and an unhindered upswing in information processing capabilities. These are but a few of the promises held by the quantum Internet, largely facilitated by quantum teleportation. Research into developing a quantum Internet, where information is transmitted via quantum states rather than classical bit counterparts, is a rapidly progressing field. The allure of a quantum Internet is primarily drawn from the principles of superposition and entanglement, foundations of quantum mechanics, which offer a whole new level of communication.

Quantum teleportation will play a critical role, allowing quantum information, such as the quantum states of particles, to be transferred from one location to another without physical transmission of the particles themselves. Compare this to the Star Trek transporter, which dematerializes an object at one location and then reassembles it at another.

The barriers to a quantum internet, however, are considerable. Current experiments have successfully teleported quantum information over 100 kilometers of free space, but practical quantum networks will likely require much more vast distances. This necessitates the development of quantum repeaters, a still-theoretical technology that could help extend the range.

Another significant challenge is the requisite control and maintenance of quantum coherence over vast networks. Currently, the technology needed for this degree of control is in its early stages, and there is much we don't yet understand about preserving coherence in large quantum systems.

9.2. Quantum Computers and Quantum Teleportation

Quantum computing, another key field where quantum teleportation is expected to play a significant role, has clearly indicated its potential to revolutionize the world of technology. Quantum computers would leverage the principles of quantum mechanics to perform calculations exponentially faster than current computing systems.

One area where quantum teleportation might further advance quantum computing is in the developing field of distributed quantum computing. By teleporting quantum information between quantum computers, it might be possible to create a quantum computing network with exponentially more processing power than any individual quantum computer.

However, just as with the quantum internet, this exponential advance in processing power comes with substantial challenges. Quantum teleportation requires highly accurate measurement and manipulation of quantum states, and any inaccuracies therein can lead to mistakes in teleported information. Furthermore, quantum computers themselves are extraordinarily sensitive to environmental disturbances, making it yet more difficult to achieve the necessary precision.

9.3. The Interstellar Impact of Quantum Teleportation

Beyond the confines of our planet, quantum teleportation may also have significant implications for space exploration and communication. The concept of instantaneous communication through entangled particles could potentially enable us to overcome the annoying communication lags that currently hinder our space exploration efforts.

However, the challenges here go even beyond those of the quantum Internet. Space is fraught with sources of noise and interference that could easily disrupt the sensitive quantum states. Moreover, to prepare and measure the entangled particles needed for teleportation, highly accurate equipment, impervious to the rigors of space travel, would be needed.

9.4. Overcoming Obstacles

Clearly, moving from our current, early experiments in quantum teleportation to the vast possibilities we envision will involve surmounting many obstacles. Technological advances will be required to achieve the necessary degree of control and accuracy. At the same time, we need a much deeper understanding of quantum physics and how to protect quantum coherence in large systems.

Quantum teleportation technology also faces challenges beyond the purely technical. As with any technology that promises to transform society so profoundly, there are moral and ethical considerations to take into account. What would a world with secure, instantaneous communication look like? It is even possible that quantum teleportation could one day enable the teleportation not just of simple quantum information but of more complex quantum systems, possibly including living organisms.

9.5. A Promising Future Despite the Hurdles

Despite these sundry challenges, the field of quantum teleportation holds an exciting future. And though these breakthroughs might appear as magic to some, we continuously strive to unfurl the mysteries behind the veil of the quantum realm. Undoubtedly, numerous breakthroughs and discoveries remain hidden in the shadows, waiting to be unearthed and augment our understanding.

Unlocking the secrets of quantum teleportation opens a myriad of unprecedented opportunities for our future. As we transcend the known limits of speed, information processing, and even the concept of being ‘there’ or ‘here’, this quantum leap promises a future replete with wonder. However, this brave new world also demands brave new thinkers, to explore this untamed frontier critically, question unremittingly, and embrace the unfolding reality of a quantum future.

In the end, the future of quantum teleportation may well reshape our understanding of the Universe, the nature of information, and the essence of reality itself. An exhilarating journey awaits us all as we venture forth onto this quantum frontier. Just remember: the journey is no less significant than the destination itself. As we witness the boundaries of scientific understanding expand before our eyes, the future is not just an anticipation, but a reality we continually create.

Chapter 10. Quenching Quantum Curiosities: Frequently Asked Questions

Teleportation is no longer a concept confined to the realm of fantastical science fiction. Instead, it is ensconced in the empirical world of quantum mechanics, a phenomenon scientists refer to as 'Quantum Teleportation'. However, let's not make the common mistake of picturing a human being beamed up from one place to another. Instead, quantum teleportation's fascination, complexity, and potential lie in the instantaneous conveyance of information.

10.1. Familiarizing with Quantum Basics

Before diving into quantum teleportation, let's get our quantum basics right. Quantum physics or quantum mechanics is a branch of physics that delves into the nature and behavior of matter and energy at the smallest scales, those of atoms and subatomic particles. It introduces some bizarre and counterintuitive concepts that defy our regular understanding of the world.

10.1.1. Q: What is Quantum Superposition?

Imagine a particle that can exist in two places simultaneously! No, this is not a trick question or a riddle. In the quantum world, particles can be in a 'superposition' of states, which means a particle can exist in multiple states at once until observed.

10.1.2. Q: What is Quantum Entanglement?

In the quantum world, things can become 'entangled'. But, this doesn't mean they get tangled up in a knot! Quantum entanglement refers to the phenomenon where pairs or groups of particles interact in ways such that the quantum state of each particle is dependent on the states of the others, no matter how far apart they are.

10.2. Dissecting Quantum Teleportation

Now, let's get closer to quantum teleportation. It is the process of transferring quantum information from one location to another, with the help of classical communication and previously shared quantum entanglement.

10.2.1. Q: How does Quantum Teleportation work?

To illustrate this, consider Alice and Bob, two famous characters often used in explanations of quantum phenomena. If Alice wants to send quantum information to Bob, she needs to prepare her system in a particular quantum state. Alice and Bob also need an entangled pair of particles. Alice then performs a measurement on her particle and the particle she wants to teleport, producing two bits of classical information. She sends this classical information to Bob. Bob uses this information to perform an operation on his half of the entangled pair, and voila, Bob's particle is now in the state Alice wanted to send!

10.2.2. Q: Why is it called Teleportation if it's about conveying information?

Granted, the term 'teleportation' is somewhat of a misnomer in this context. The 'teleportation' part of quantum teleportation isn't implying that physical particles are being transported from location A to location B. Instead, it is the quantum information the particle holds that is 'teleported' or sent instantaneously.

10.3. Quantum Teleportation versus Classical Communication

Upon first glance, quantum teleportation seems similar to classical communication, but a more profound look reveals striking differences.

10.3.1. Q: How is Quantum Teleportation different from Classical Communication?

In classical communication, information can be sent from point A to point B, but it can never exceed the speed of light. In contrast, quantum teleportation leverages entanglement, a non-local property in quantum mechanics, to transfer information instantaneously.

10.3.2. Q: Can Quantum Teleportation enable faster-than-light communication?

In a word: no. Even though quantum entanglement allows instantaneous correlation between distant particles, relaying usable information also involves classical communication, which cannot exceed light speed.

10.4. Practical Applications of Quantum Teleportation

Quantum teleportation is more than just an exciting concept. It forms the backbone of many futuristic technologies.

10.4.1. Q: What are the possible applications of Quantum Teleportation?

Quantum teleportation could form the backbone of future technologies such as quantum computing and quantum internet, where the ability to send quantum information is critical.

10.4.2. Q: What is the furthest distance that Quantum Teleportation has been achieved?

To date, the record for quantum teleportation distance was set by researchers in 2017, successfully teleporting a photon over 1400 kilometers using a satellite.

Chapter 11. Quantum Teleportation: A Reality or a Far-fetched Dream?

While we've come a long way in understanding quantum teleportation, much remains to be mastered. But, as history has repeatedly shown us, science is a relentless explorer. Today's fiction could very well pave the path for tomorrow's reality.

Chapter 12. Further Quantum Leaps: Exploring Beyond Teleportation

Quantum mechanics, though enthralling in its apparent contradiction of reality as we know it, extends far beyond the principle of teleportation. It is an inexhaustible box of seemingly impossible tricks that reshape our understanding of the universe. As we set our sights past quantum teleportation, prepare to venture further into a realm where the strange is ordinary, and the impossible does not exist.

12.1. How Quantum Computing Works

A crucial leap beyond teleportation is the quantum computer, capable of processing vast amounts of data simultaneously, thereby exceeding traditional computers in specific tasks. Keep your slide rules and calculators at bay as we delved into simplistic explanations of these complex processes.

The central crux of quantum computing is quantum bits or "qubits." Unlike the binary "bits" of traditional computing, which are either a 0 or a 1, qubits can be both 0 and 1 at the same time – a property known as superposition. This state of superposition allows quantum computers to conduct exponentially more calculations simultaneously, adding a dimension of processing power that is impossible for classical computers.

Quantum computers also use quantum entanglement, allowing qubits to become interlinked and maintain a relationship, regardless of the distance that separates them. Because of entanglement, changing the state of one qubit will instantaneously change the state of the other, which is a critical feature of quantum computing.

12.2. Quantum Field Theory

Quantum Field Theory (QFT) combines quantum mechanics' principles with the concept of fields—a system of values assigned to every point in space. This theory provides the framework for understanding particles like photons, electrons, and quarks – the constituents of atoms. However, QFT is not just about particles. It also predicts "virtual particles" created in the quantum "field" and annihilated in less time than we can measure.

This may seem like a fantastical account, but it is proven in reality – the Casimir effect. Dutch physicists showed that if two mirrors are brought exceptionally close together in a vacuum, they will attract each other. This phenomenon arises because the area between the mirrors can only accommodate virtual particles of specific wavelengths, creating a discrepancy in the virtual particle pressure and causing an attraction.

12.3. Quantum Entanglement and Spooky Action

Quantum mechanics deem any two particles can be "entangled"— what Einstein referred to as "spooky action at a distance." When particles become entangled, they remain connected such that actions performed on one particle have an immediate effect on the other, regardless of the distance separating them.

Quantum entanglement forms the backbone of quantum teleportation and quantum computing. However, it also positions itself in the development of quantum cryptography and quantum communications, offering a prospect at an ultra-secure means of transmitting informational data.

12.4. The Quantum Multiverse

The multiverse theory opposes the traditional belief in a single universe. Instead, it hypothesizes the existence of numerous (even infinite) universes, each having its distinct laws of physics. While it may seem like a fanciful science fiction trope, the multiverse theory originated from quantum mechanics.

Physicist Hugh Everett first proposed this "Many-Worlds Interpretation" in 1957, suggesting that all possible quantum events can occur in some "branch" of the universe. The theory does not ignore any possibilities; instead, each one exists in a diverse universe.

12.5. Quantum Gravity

Reality warps under the gravity of celestial bodies, as theorized by Einstein in his general theory of relativity. Quantum mechanics, however, is yet to integrate this understanding. The pursuit to reconcile gravity with quantum mechanics—dubbed quantum gravity—remains an unsolved mystery in theoretical physics.

Several theories have attempted to bridge this chasm. One of the most prominent is string theory, which postulates that all particles are one-dimensional strings rather than zero-dimensional points. Different vibrations of the strings correspond to different particles, and fundamentally, gravity is one such vibration.

Taking a leap beyond quantum teleportation allows us to broach the frontiers of science and delve deeper into our universe's mystifying paradoxes. These further leaps imbue us with a sanctified understanding, enabling us to see our universe through a renewed lens. As we step into the morrow of scientific understanding, these tenets of quantum science promise to carry humanity forward into an era of unrivaled technological prowess and unprecedented insights into our universe's enigmas.

www.ingramcontent.com/pod-product-compliance
Lightning Source LLC
LaVergne TN
LVHW051624050326
832903LV00033B/4647